Hungry Bugs
by Ruth Owen

Editorial consultant: Mitch Cronick

CONTENTS

Words in **bold** are explained in the glossary.

Let's eat!

Hungry bugs like to eat.

Butterfly

Slurp!

Beetle

Munch!

Chomp!

Praying mantis

5

Aphids

Aphids suck **sap** from plants.

Aphids

Ladybirds

Ladybirds eat aphids.

Aphid

Ladybird

A ladybird eats 50 aphids in a day!

Leaf-cutter ants

These ants cut up leaves with their **jaws**.

Leaf

Leaf-cutter ant

They make ant food with the leaves.

Jaws

Honeybees

Honeybees suck **nectar** from flowers.

Honeybee

Yummy honey!

Honeybees make **honey** with nectar.

Honeybee

Bee **larvae** eat the honey.

Larvae

We can eat the honey too!

Honey

Munch crunch lunch!

Caterpillars eat plants.

Caterpillars

Butterflies

Caterpillars turn into butterflies!

4

3

1

2

Butterfly

Butterflies suck nectar from flowers.

19

Dung beetle

This **dung** beetle eats elephant poo!

Poo

Elephant

Dung beetle

Glossary

dung
A word for animal poo.

honey
A thick, sweet food made by bees.

jaws
Parts of an ant's head that it uses to bite.

larvae
The young (babies)
of some bugs.

nectar
Sweet, runny stuff that
comes from flowers.

sap
Runny stuff
made by plants.

Index

Publisher: Melissa Fairley
Studio Manager: Sara Greasley
Editor: Emma Dods
Designer: Trudi Webb
Production Controller: Ed Green
Production Manager: Suzy Kelly

ISBN 978 1 84898 113 3

Copyright © ticktock Entertainment Ltd 2009
First published in Great Britain in 2009 by ticktock Media Ltd.,
The Old Sawmill, 103 Goods Station Road, Tunbridge Wells, Kent TN1 2DP

Printed in China
9 8 7 6 5 4 3 2 1

Picture credits (t=top, b=bottom, c=centre, l=left, r=right, OFC= outside front cover, OBC=outside back cover): iStock: 8, 23t. Jupiter Images: 15. Shutterstock: OFC, 1, 2, 4–5 all, 6–7, 9, 10–11, 12, 13, 16–17 all, 18–19 all, 20–21, 21, 22t, 22b, 23b, OBC. Gary K. Smith/FLPA: 14–15.

Every effort has been made to trace the copyright holders, and we apologize in advance for any unintentional omissions. We would be pleased to insert the appropriate acknowledgements in any subsequent edition of this publication.